mAttEd fuR ❖ You hAVe a LiTTL

kes ❖ H　　　　　　　❖ LeT

th of Oi　　　　　　　E TuNa

hAnDLeS ❖ whAt iS THat SmeLL?

❖ LiSten AnD FoLLOw uS ❖ I s

❖ mY MezuZah ❖ HAnukCaTS ❖

mAttEd fuR ❖ You hAVe a LiTTL

kes ❖ HaNukkAh MeSSeS ❖ LeT

th of OiL ❖ WE WAnT soME TuNa

hAnDLeS ❖ whAt iS THat SmeLL?

❖ LiSten AnD FoLLOw uS ❖ I s

❖ mY MezuZah ❖ HAnukCaTS

HaNuKCaTs

and Other Traditional Jewish Songs for Cats

HaNuKCaTS
and Other Traditional Jewish Songs for Cats

by Laurie Loughlin

illustrated by Mary Ross

Chronicle Books * San Francisco

The author and publisher have made every reasonable
attempt to determine that the songs parodied in this work
are in the public domain.

Printed in Hong Kong.

Book and cover design: Leeb & Sons, Carrie Leeb

Library of Congress Cataloging-in-Publication Data
Loughlin, Laurie
Hanukcats : and other traditional Jewish songs for cats /
by Laurie Loughlin ; illustrated by Mary Ross.
p. cm.
ISBN: 0-8118-0798-3
1. Cats—Humor. 2. Hanukkah—Humor 3. Jewish—Humor.
PN6231.C23L685   1994
636.8'0207—dc20   94-1393
                                                CIP

Distributed in Canada by Raincoast Books,
8680 Cambie Street, Vancouver, B.C. V6P 6M9

10 9 8 7 6 5 4 3 2

Chronicle Books
85 Second Street
San Francisco, CA 94105

For my mother and father, who have always believed in miracles.

My thanks to:

* Cantor Bernard Gutcheon for sharing his music and advising me

* Carrie Leeb for her fine feline design

* Mary Ann Gilderbloom for spreading the meow

* Lee Floersheimer for her research assistance

* my "menshen," Penelope and Greta

tABLE of

coNtentS

It's NOT ENOUGH Thank

bone. And the

matzoh bread.

your good inten

It's not enough.

It won't suffice.

We're still hun

more food this

you for the shank

haroset and

We do appreciate

tions, but

("Dayenu"–for Passover)

gry.   We need

very minute!

Kmart, KmArt

Kmart, Kmart, go there, please.
Buy me shampoo that kills fleas.
Hanukkah is glee, eight presents for me.
Purr, purr, purr, purr, purr, purr, purr,
Purr, purr, purr, purr, purr, purr, purr,
Hanukkah is glee, eight presents for me.

How about a scratching board,
Foam balls dangling from a cord?
Catnip birds and mice would be very nice.
Purr, purr, purr, purr, purr, purr, purr,
Purr, purr, purr, purr, purr, purr, purr,
Hanukkah is glee, eight presents for me.

Get a collar that will fit,
One designed by Jaclyn Smith,
Cat rugs that won't snag, and the paper bag!
Purr, purr, purr, purr, purr, purr, purr,
Purr, purr, purr, purr, purr, purr, purr,
Hanukkah is glee, eight presents for me.

("Kemah, Kemah")

mAttEd fuR

Matted fur all over me,
Smoothness now my coat lacks.
Being long-haired certainly
Has its cosmetic drawbacks.
Knots that thwart the hairbrush,
All attempts to tame my tress,
It just makes me feel so blah
'Cause I'll look bad for Hanukkah.
It just makes me feel so blah
'Cause I'll look bad for Hanukkah.

("Ma'oz Tsur")

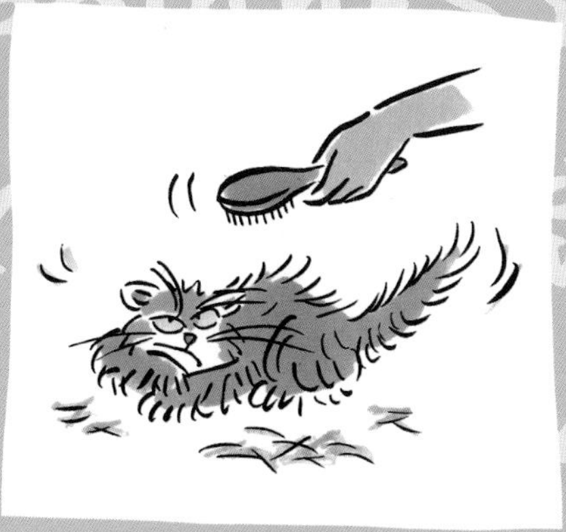

You hAve
a LiTtLe DrEideL

You have a little dreidel
With which I'd like to play.
The minute you're not looking,
I'll spirit it away.

Dreidel, dreidel, dreidel,
With which I'd like to play,
Dreidel, dreidel, dreidel,
I'll spirit it away.

I have a lovely body
With legs so long and thin.
My paw will fling the dreidel
And make it spin, spin, spin.

Dreidel, dreidel, dreidel,
My legs are long and thin.
Dreidel, dreidel, dreidel,
I'll make it spin, spin, spin.

I don't care what it stops on,
Nun, gimel, he, or shin.
I make up my own rules, and
Whichever one, I win!

Dreidel, dreidel, dreidel,
Nun, gimel, he, or shin,
Dreidel, dreidel, dreidel,
Whichever one, I win!

("I Have a Little Dreidel")

tiny Bow Tiny bow

I can pull it out,

I will jump right

upon your lap,

And that tiny

I will jump up

And that tiny

atop your dress,

I guess.

("Hi 'Ne Bo")

bow I'll snap!

on your lap,

bow I'll snap!

oH, YaRMuLkes

Oh, yarmulkes! Oh, yarmulkes!
Our precious little caps,
We wear you to the synagogue
And also taking naps.
Cotton, wool, and satin,
Opaques and sheers,
When perched atop our heads, they
Complement our ears.

In neons and pastels,
They won't blow off even in a breeze.
They decorate our uppers.
We put them on for suppers
And sometimes even when we're climbing trees.

Oh, yarmulkes! Oh, yarmulkes!
You helped make history
When we reclaimed our holy Temple
Back in B.C.E.
After all we did, it's
So annoying that
Nobody ever mentions
The Maccabees were cats!

In neons and pastels,
We flowed like a rainbow down the hill.
We frightened Antiochus.
His legions could not knock us.
We love you, yarmulkes, and always will!

("Oy Hanuka")

HaNukkAh MeSSeS

I goofed today in the den,
Lost my breakfast shortly after ten.
I left my mark upon the brand-new rug
And on presents so brightly wrapped
For Hanukkah. Uuh-oh.

I goofed at lunchtime once more,
Knocked a pan of latkes on the floor.
Hot oil spilled across linoleum
Which was warping as it flowed.
Everyone saw me, too. Uuh-oh.

I goofed this evening again,
Swiped the shammes, buried it and then
Came back inside where Uncle Clyde
Some wax he spied
On my whiskers. Uuh-oh.

("Chanuka Blessings")

LeT me gloAt

I am a star. Let me gloat, emote.
Let me gloat, emote. You can dote.
Let me gloat, emote. You can dote.

You shall attempt to please me.
You shall attempt to please me.
You shall attempt to please me,
Please me for Hanukkah.

("L'Vivot")

JuSt ONe NiGht's WoRth of OiL

Just one night's worth of oil
Could we light for our toil,
Our Maccabee win to celebrate.
By a miracle one night turned into eight.
Our Maccabee win to celebrate,
By a miracle one night turned into eight.

We were fueled from on high.
When our feat caught His eye,
One lampful was turned into vats.
Yes, and that's how we became the Hanukcats!
One lampful was turned into vats.
Yes, and that's how we became the Hanukcats!

("Y'Ladim Baneyrot")

WE WANT SOME TUNA AND CHICKEN

We want some tu

We want some tu

We want some tu

We want some tu

Beef would be ni

(Repeat several times, increa

the tempo each time.)

na and chicken.

na and chicken.

na and chicken.

na, chicken,

ce, too.

sing

HaVE a buRRito

Part 1 (a) Have a burrito.
                Beef bits are neato
                Especially when you
                Drop them on the floor.
                Gefilte fish are
                Something we wish for.
                Give us a dish or
                Leave an open jar.

Part 2   We'll do the kitchen floor.
                Don't worry 'bout that chore.
                We'll clean up every crumb
                Like all good cats should.
                We love the holidays.
                It's not a passing phase.
                Big celebrations mean
                That we get more food.

                Me-ow. Meow. Meow. Meow. Meow!

                ("Hava Nagila"–for celebrations)

Part 3   Now is the time to start the seder.
          Please don't decide to make it later.
          Now is the time to start the seder.
          Please don't decide to make it later.
          Aren't you starved?
          Wouldn't you like
          To sink your teeth into a feast?

Part 1 (b) We know Socks Clinton
            Spends his days blintzin'
            With his friend, Chelsea,
            On the White House lawn.
            With Justice Ginzburg
            He shares some linzer,
            The only cat to
            See the Supreme Court.

          Repeat parts 2 & 3

I've got Love handles

I've got love handles 'round my tum.
Hanukkah is here.
I lick my chops and dig right in
When those treats appear.
Pat my love handles, one by one,
Eating is such fun.
I'll stretch and yawn and go to sleep
When Hanukkah is done.

("Shine Little Candles")

what is That SmeLL?

What is that smell
That floats from the kitchen?
What is that smell?
Whether a chop,
A rump, or a brisket,
It smells swell.

Open the door
So we can get more
Of that aroma.
What is that smell?
Oh, pray, won't you tell us
Right away.

Aaah. . .
Left to our imaginations
Aaah. . .
We will conjure up temptations
Aaah. . .
Picturing a plate of every kind.
Won't you help restore our peace of mind?

(Repeat as a round.)

("Mi Y'Malel")

32

Silly one

Try to catch your

Hanukkitten, you

When to turn and

turn. ♡ I will give

To my life great

Circling 'round

Hearts together,

spin, spin, spin.

tail again.

("S'Vivon")

will learn

not to

you everything.

joy you bring.

this special time,

yours and mine.

in a ROw
I Light you

In a row, in a row,
In a row I light you.
In a row I light you,
Eight pretty candles blue.
Hanukkah will end,
But not its inner glow.
Eight candles represent
The joy we've come to know.
Let's dance the hora,
Join in a circle of paws.
Hanukcat menorah,
It's mine and yours.

("Haneyrot Halala")

Listen

And
FoLLOw
uS

Listen and just follow us.
There are things we must discuss.
Hanukkah is on the way,
But have you hugged your cat today?
You get busy and forget
To take time to pet your pet.
Now, what is all this mishegoss?
We still need you to love us.

Listen and just follow us.
There are things we must discuss.
Hanukkah is on the way,
Big preparations every day.
All these special meals you do,
We demand a bite or two.
You can't expect us to stay calm.
So much food just turns us on!

("Listen and Follow Me")

I sURe miSs hiM

I sure miss him.
He is my buddy.
He went to college.
My life's all bollixed.
We used to run and play,
But then he went away.
He's coming home for Hanukkah today!

I sure miss him.
Of all the family,
He is the one who
I'm most attached to.
Now I can hardly wait
Till he comes through the gate.
He's coming home for Hanukkah today!

("Al Hanisim")

it's me you picked

It's me you picked to be your cat.
I'm glad I'm not alone,
And finally I will get to spend
A Hanukkah at home.
La la la la la la
La la la la la la
La la la la la la
Hanukkah at home.
La la la la la la
La la la la la la
La la la la la la
Hanukkah at home.

All cats will do their best to keep
The holy days on their own,
But it's so nice when they can spend
A Hanukkah at home.
La la la la la la
La la la la la la
La la la la la la
Hanukkah at home.
La la la la la la
La la la la la la
La la la la la la
Hanukkah at home.

("Mi Ze Hidlik")

t's ME You Pi
e YOUR cAt. I'
m n
E, a
will
spe
anukkah at h
ll cats will do
Keep thE Hol

MY MezuZAh

My mezuzah is fastened to the door.
I like to chew it 'cause that is what it's for.
It's got my toothmark.
It's looking so sharp
On this the first day of Hanukkah.

My mezuzah is fastened to the door.
I like to chew it 'cause that is what it's for.
It's got two toothmarks.
It's looking so sharp
On this the second day of Hanukkah.

(Repeat, changing the numbers to the
appropriate day of Hanukkah.)

("My Candles")

HANUKCATS   Hanuk

Honor those today

Hanukcats, 🐾Who

Hanukcats, Hanu

sleek, and strong.

Hanukcats, Hanu

Who were never

cats, Hanukcats,

🐾 Hanukcats,

have led the way.

kcats, 🐾 Stubborn,

kcats,

wrong!

("Hanukah")

It's NOT ENOugH ❋ KMaRt, KMART

DrEidEL ❋ tiny BoW ❋ oH, YaRM

ME gLOAt ❋ JuSt ONe NiGht'S W

❋ HaVE a buRRito ❋ I've gOt Lo

iLLY ONe ❋ in a ROW I Light yoU

miSs hiM ❋ it's me You PicKEC

It's NOT ENOugH ❋ KMaRt, KMART

DrEidEL ❋ tiny BoW ❋ oH, YaRM

ME gLOAt ❋ JuSt ONe NiGht'S W

❋ HaVE a buRRito ❋ I've gOt Lo

iLLY ONe ❋ in a ROW I Light yoU

miSs hiM ❋ it's me You PicKEC